My Life:
Based on the Book
Gifted Hands

Also by Ben Carson, M.D.

One Vote
(with Candy Carson)

One Nation
(with Candy Carson)

America the Beautiful
(with Candy Carson)

Gifted Hands
(with Cecil Murphey)

Think Big
(with Cecil Murphey)

Take the Risk
(with Gregg Lewis)

The Big Picture
(with Gregg Lewis)

You Have a Brain
*(with Gregg Lewis and
Deborah Shaw Lewis)*

My Life:
Based on the Book
Gifted Hands

BEN CARSON, M.D.

ZONDERVAN

ZONDERVAN

My Life
Copyright © 2015 by Ben Carson
Based on the Book *Gifted Hands*

This title is also available as a Zondervan ebook.
Visit www.zondervan.com/ebooks.

Requests for information should be addressed to:
Zondervan, *3900 Sparks Dr. SE, Grand Rapids, Michigan 49546*

ISBN 978-0-310-34451-3

Published in association with Yates & Yates, www.yates2.com.

Edited by Lyn Cryderman and Becky Jen
Cover design: Curt Diepenhorst
Cover photography: Jana Cruder Photography
Interior design: Beth Shagene

First printing May 2015 / Printed in the United States of America

Contents

CHAPTER 1

"Why Can't We Just Forgive Him?"

Just like that, he was gone.

When my mother announced that my dad wasn't going to live with us anymore, I thought I must have done something bad to make him want to leave. Then, when my mom said he had to leave because *he* had done something bad, the answer seemed so easy to my eight-year-old self.

"Then we can just forgive him, right?" I asked.

I was too young to understand the bad things that Daddy had done. To me, he was my dad, an affectionate and caring man who did fun things with my brother, Curtis, and me. I used to love to sit on his lap and play this game. With my little hands I would try to push down the big veins on the backs of his large, strong hands. No matter how hard I pushed, the veins would always pop back, and Daddy would laugh and say, "Guess you're just not strong enough."

I loved my dad.

Sometimes he would bring us presents for no special reason. "I just thought you'd like this," he would say as he handed me a box, his dark eyes twinkling at my excitement. He wasn't around a lot, but when he was, he always made me happy. When I knew he was on his way home, I would sit by the window and watch, and when I saw him strolling down our alley, I would run out to him screaming, "Daddy! Daddy!" Then he would grab me up in his arms and carry me the rest of the way home.

And then he was gone.

As my mother tried to explain why he could never come back, I sobbed in her lap. She tried to comfort me. I couldn't imagine life without Daddy and pestered her for weeks, trying to make her change her mind. I pleaded with her, trying every argument my tender little mind could come up with:

"With Daddy gone, we won't have any money— what'll we do?"

"If you let him come back, I know he'll be good."

"Mothers and fathers are supposed to stay together."

What I didn't know was that my father had another "wife," and together they were raising a whole other family. He also struggled with drugs, but I didn't know about any of this at that time because my mother kept it from us. His behavior must have hurt her deeply, but we never knew. She carried this burden alone because she wanted to protect us from the truth about my father.

Every night when I said my prayers, I asked God to help Mother and Dad get back together. I desperately wanted us to be a family again, but after a few weeks, I stopped praying. My mom told me later that Curtis and I struggled with a lot of pain during that time, but to be honest, I don't recall anything other than Dad's leaving. I guess that's how I learned to handle my feelings. I just tried to forget them.

One thing I do remember is that we never had enough money. Even before Daddy left, we were never well off, but without his paycheck, we barely scraped by. Every time I asked my mother for something like a candy bar or a new toy, her answer was always the same: "We don't have the money, Bennie." I could tell from the look on her face that it hurt her to not be able to buy us the things that other kids had, so after a while I quit asking.

I didn't know it then, but even though my dad was supposed to send us money, he seldom did. Maybe that's why a few times we went with Mother to the big courthouse. In spite of his lack of support, my mom seldom uttered a critical word about my dad, and that's probably why I never held a grudge against him. Rather than focus on him, Mother set her mind on making sure we were a happy family, even if it was just the three of us. Despite her lack of education and having to fend for us all by herself, she never complained. Countless times she reassured me: "Bennie, we're going to be fine."

It wasn't easy for Curtis and me to grow up without a dad, but it was even harder for Mother to carry the burden of providing for us all by herself. Before my dad left, Mother was always there, but now she had to work and be away a lot. Her dedication and sacrifice had a big impact on me, which is why I begin with her. Sonya Carson. The earliest, strongest, and most important force in my life. The only way I can tell my story is to begin with hers.

CHAPTER 2

The Driving Force

I almost felt sorry for the school counselor who got an unexpected visit from Mother.

Back in the day, schools tracked students according to their abilities, and the junior high that my brother Curtis attended placed him in the vocational curriculum rather than the college-prep curriculum. His grades were good enough for the college curriculum, but this was a predominately white school, and Mother was convinced that the counselor had made the fairly common assumption that blacks were incapable of college work. So Mother headed straight for the counselor's office the next day.

"My son Curtis is going to college," she told the counselor. "I don't want him taking any vocational courses."

Curtis immediately became college material and was placed on the college-prep curriculum.

That's my mom—a strong woman who does not allow the system to dictate her life. Today we would describe her as a classic type-A personality. Driven, hardworking, refusing to settle for anything but the best. She was also a big-picture woman, intuitively knowing exactly what needed to be done in any situation. Some of that rubbed off on me, though I wasn't always open to her constant prodding to do my best. In fact, at times she

could seem demanding, even heartless. The word
quit wasn't in her vocabulary, and she tried her best
to banish it from mine. I can't tell you how many
times I heard her say, "You can do it, Bennie!" or
her favorite, "Just ask the Lord, and he'll help you."

Being kids, Curtis and I often resented her constant pushing, but over the years it took hold. We
started to believe that we could do anything we
chose to do. I guess you could say she brainwashed
us—in a good way. Even today, when faced with
something that seems impossible, I can still hear
my mother's voice: "You can do it, Bennie. Don't
you stop believing that for one second."

Mother may have had only a third-grade education, but she was the driving force in our lives.
Her frugality allowed us to own our own home.
In contrast, my father placed more emphasis on
looking good, having nice things, and being liked.
Both of my parents had come from large families—
Mother had twenty-three siblings, and Daddy had
thirteen. After they got married in Chattanooga,
they moved to Detroit like so many other laborers
in search of work. My father got a job at the Cadil-
lac plant and, believe it or not, served as a minister
at a small Baptist church.

. . .

Several months after Mother told us that Daddy
would not be coming home again, it started.

"I'm going to be gone for a few days to visit
some relatives."

When we asked if we were going too, the answer was always the same. "No, I have to go alone. Besides, you have school. I've already arranged for you to stay with the neighbors."

What we didn't know was that "visiting relatives" meant she was checking herself into a mental institution. The separation and divorce had brought on periods of severe depression, and somehow she had the inner strength to know she needed help. This happened several times, and each time, she would be gone for several weeks. We never knew because she never wanted us to know. But our neighbors knew, and it became a hot topic of gossip. Mother kept her head high and did her best to provide for us, but eventually it became clear that she couldn't keep up with the expenses of living in our home. So she rented it out, packed us up, and headed to Boston where we moved in with her older sister, Jean Avery, and her husband, William.

The Averys became like another set of parents to Curtis and me, showering us with much-needed love and affection. For another year or so Mother continued to go away for psychiatric treatment, but the Averys always reassured us that she was doing fine. Though we missed her, Aunt Jean and Uncle William treated us so well that we grew to like our living arrangement. They handled the situation so well that we never knew how difficult things really were for Mother.

Despite being abandoned by friends, talked about behind her back, moving out of state, and struggling with near-paralyzing depression, she never let on just how lonely and sad she was. And she never gave up.

Because that's who Sonya Carson is.

CHAPTER 3

"I'm Just Dumb"

B oston was nothing like Detroit.

Instead of our own home, we lived in what used to be called a tenement building, basically a dilapidated structure in which a lot of families lived. Instead of dogs and cats, rats roamed our neighborhood. They were bigger than cats! They mostly scurried around the piles of garbage in the alley, but sometimes they'd get inside our apartment, joining the ever-present cockroaches. No matter what Mother tried, she couldn't get rid of those nasty roaches.

You might think we hated our new surroundings, but within a few weeks they seemed normal. Mother worked all the time, cleaning rich people's homes, but when she got back, no matter how tired she was, she would quiz us about school. She made it clear that education came ahead of everything. That, and the kindness of the Averys, made life in Boston seem pretty good, in spite of our poor surroundings.

In fact, living in Boston may have been the best part of my childhood. For one thing, that year I had the best Christmas ever. Maybe the Averys and my mom were trying to compensate for the absence of my father, but they smothered us with presents. What eight-year-old boy wouldn't be thrilled to get a scale-model 1959 Buick? But the best gift of all was a chemistry set. I played with that for hours, mixing chemicals and conducting experiments. I was fascinated with the test tubes and litmus paper and how you could make a liquid change colors. Sometimes I'd mix the wrong chemicals, and a horrible smell would drift through the apartment, annoying everyone else but making me laugh like crazy.

But even better was the day I made the decision to follow Jesus. We were Seventh-day Adventists, so we went to church on Saturdays. One Saturday morning at our church on Burns Avenue, Pastor Ford illustrated his sermon with a story about a missionary couple being pursued by robbers, but they escaped by hiding in a small split in the side of a cliff.

"They hid in the cleft of that rock, and God protected them," he told us.

At the close of the sermon he led the congregation in the hymn, "He Hideth My Soul in the Cleft of the Rock," pausing between verses to tell us that if we placed our faith in the Lord, we would always be safe.

That's all I needed to hear. Even though I was only eight, I walked up to the front of the church to accept Pastor Ford's invitation to turn my life over to Jesus Christ. Curtis joined me, and a few weeks later we were baptized. With my newfound faith, I began thinking about what I wanted to do with my life. At church we often heard stories about missionary doctors in far-off places like Africa and India, where they would treat sick people in remote villages. That's when I decided to be a doctor.

When I told my mom, she looked me straight in the eye and said, "If you ask the Lord for something and believe he will do it, then it will happen."

"I believe I can be a doctor," I responded.

"Then you'll be a doctor."

Just like that. Her simple faith convinced me that I really *could* be a doctor.

■■■

After three years in Boston, Mother's finances improved, so she moved us back to Detroit, hoping to return to our original house on Deacon Street. Even though that house was tiny, she still couldn't afford to live there, so we moved to the top floor of an apartment building in an industrial area. Still, it was a step up from our place in Boston. Mother worked as many as three jobs at a time, mostly working for wealthy people. When she came home at night, she'd school us on how these rich folk lived, adding, "You boys can live that way too if you want to." She was always pushing us to higher goals and values, especially the value of education.

Unfortunately, I was the dumbest kid in my class.

■■■

Higgins Elementary School was predominantly white, and the fifth graders I joined were way ahead of me. And they let me know it. After every test, someone would invariably yell out, "Hey, Carson, another zero?" Those words stung, but I never let them know it. I began to accept my spot at the bottom of the class. Worse yet, I also began to believe that black kids just weren't as smart as white kids.

I'll never forget the math quiz that turned out to be the worst school experience of my life. In those days, students corrected each other's quizzes, then handed them back to the owner. The teacher, Mrs. Williamson, then called out each student's name, and we were supposed to respond with the number of questions we got right. As she started calling out names, I dreaded having to let the whole classroom know my score.

It wasn't long before she got to me. "Benjamin?"

Wishing I could disappear, I mumbled my answer.

"Nine? Why Benjamin, that's wonderful!"

Being praised for failing a quiz was bad enough, but the girl behind me, who had graded my test, made sure Mrs. Williamson—and everyone else—heard me properly. "He said *none*, not nine!" she snickered as the entire classroom erupted in laughter.

To her credit, Mrs. Williamson scolded them, but the damage was done. I really *was* stupid. I knew it. They knew it. And it hurt. The only thing I could think to do was to make them think that I didn't care, that their laughter didn't bother me, even though I felt like crying. So I did what was becoming a common response to my own shortcomings. I plastered a big, carefree smile on my face.

I likely would have accepted the fact that as a black kid I would never amount to anything, except for two things that happened that year that changed everything.

CHAPTER 4

A Change of Vision

I took my first step up from the bottom of my class by failing another test. Only this time it was an eye test. Midway through the fifth grade, every student took a compulsory eye exam, and I couldn't read anything below that top line with the largest letters. Once again, I felt so stupid; the boy ahead of me could read the entire chart.

Obviously, I needed glasses, which the school provided. When I went to get fitted for them, the doctor said, "Son, your vision is so bad you could easily be labeled handicapped."

My brain wasn't the problem; it was my eyes. And once I got my glasses, things started to improve. I was thrilled when the midterm report cards came out and I got a *D* in math. That may not seem like a big deal, but when all you've ever gotten were failing grades, a *D* gave you hope. But even better than the *D* was the praise I got from my teacher, Mrs. Williamson.

"Benjamin," she said with a bright smile, "on the whole, you're doing much better."

I'm not sure if it was her words or her smile, but having a teacher's encouragement made me want to do even better. For the first time since entering Higgins School, I knew I could do better than some of my classmates.

With Mother, it was a different story. "Bennie, I'm proud of you for getting a better grade. And why shouldn't you? You're smart, Bennie. But you can't settle for just barely passing. You can make the top grade in your class in math."

"But Mother," I groaned, "at least I didn't fail."

To Mother, that wasn't good enough. "You can still do better," she insisted, adding, "and I'm going to help you."

When I learned how Mother was going to help me, my heart sank. But looking back, it was exactly what I needed. If getting glasses was the first positive thing that happened to me in school, Mother's plan was the second. She sprung it on me one evening not long after I brought home my improved report card.

"Bennie, since you're doing better in math, you're going to keep improving, and here's how you're going to do it. First, you're going to memorize your times tables."

I couldn't believe my ears. "I can't possibly learn that much," I protested.

That's when Mother stood a little taller and gave me that look. "I only went through the third grade, but I know them all the way through my twelves."

I knew it would do no good to argue with her, and I started to turn away as she unveiled the rest of her plan. "You can do it, Bennie. Work on them tonight, and then, when you come home from school tomorrow and I get home from work, we'll review them together." Then came her final shot. "Besides, you're not to go outside to play after school tomorrow until you've learned all those tables."

I didn't realize it at the time, but Mother was purposefully setting my sights high. I was almost in tears. It would be impossible to learn all those tables in such a short time. But Mother believed in me and knew that if I applied myself, I could do it. And somehow I did. I just kept repeating those times tables over and over and, just as she promised, I learned them.

Almost overnight, math became easier, and my grades soared. I'll never forget how I felt the first time I got every question right on a math quiz. There were twenty-four questions, and when Mrs. Williamson called my name to get my score, I practically shouted— "Twenty-four!"

For the first time in my life I enjoyed going to school. No one made fun of me or called me a dummy anymore. But Mother's plan was just getting started. She wanted me to get the best grades in every class, not just math. That was fine with me—I just didn't like her method.

"You boys watch too much television," she told us one day. "From now on you may only watch three programs a week."

No matter how much Curtis and I protested, Mother held her ground. In fact, she had already decided how we would spend all that extra time. "You're going to go to the library, check out books, and read two per week," she told us. "At the end of each week, you'll give me a report on both books."

It was bad enough that I'd have to miss my favorite television programs, but I hadn't read an entire book in my life. I didn't believe I could do it, but Mother believed I could. It was all part of her plan. "Bennie, if you can read, you can learn just about anything."

Mother had such faith in Curtis and me. Almost daily she would say to me, "Bennie, you can do anything you set yourself to do." Her confidence in me helped me believe in myself. But not everyone approved of her methods. Some of Mother's friends criticized her for being too strict and warned that we would turn on her.

"They can hate me if they want," she answered, "but they're going to get an education just the same."

Mom's plan began to work. Because I loved animals and nature, I chose library books on those topics. My science teacher, Mr. Jack, noticed my interest and began giving me special projects, such as helping other students identify rocks, animals, and fish. I became the fifth-grade expert on anything to do with science. But because I read so much, I started getting better grades in all my subjects. My vocabulary improved along with my comprehension, and soon I became the best student in math when we did story problems.

My newfound confidence instilled a desire I had never experienced before. I wanted to be the best. It started when Bobby Farmer, the smartest kid in class, answered our history teacher's question about flax. I had no idea what flax was, but Bobby explained to the class what it was, where it was grown, and how women spun its fibers into linen. Suddenly I realized that, just like Mother said, I could learn about flax or anything else just by reading. I thought it must be really fun to know you're the smartest kid in class, so on that day, I decided the only way to know how that would feel would be to actually become the smartest.

I kept reading all through the next summer, and when sixth grade began, Bobby was still the smartest—but I was gaining on him. Throughout the sixth grade I continued to improve, and by the time I entered the seventh grade, I was at the top of the class! The same kids who once made fun of me now came to me for help with their schoolwork. Thanks to Mother's influence, I had earned their respect. More importantly, I respected myself. No longer did I just want to be better than others; I wanted to be the best I could be—for me.

Doing so well in the predominately white Wilson School helped to erase the stereotype of blacks being intellectually inferior. At the same time, it introduced me to prejudice. Three incidents come to mind.

Curtis and I used to hop trains to get to school, even though it was dangerous and we knew we weren't supposed to. The train tracks ran parallel to our route to school, so it just seemed like a fun thing to do. Curtis, being older and braver, hopped the faster trains while I opted for the slower ones. One day when Curtis wasn't with me, a group of older boys—all white—blocked my path. One of them carried a big stick.

"Hey, you! Nigger boy!"

I froze, frightened and silent. The boy with the stick whacked me across my shoulder as the other boys called me every vile name you could imagine. Since they were all much bigger than I was, fighting back or running was out of the question.

"You know you nigger kids aren't supposed to be going to Wilson," the leader of the group sneered. "If we ever catch you again, we're going to kill you. You understand that, nigger boy?"

Fear grabbed at my throat, but I managed to answer, "Yes."

"Then get out of here as fast as you can. Next time, we'll kill you!"

I never hopped a train again, and I never told Mother.

The next incident should have been a celebration. At the end of the year, the principal handed out certificates to the top student in each grade. I won it in the second grade as Curtis won his for the ninth grade. I then went on to win it for both the eighth grade and the ninth. At the assembly when I won it for the ninth grade, the teacher who presented it to me used the occasion to berate the white kids for letting me, a black kid, win.

Of course, I was hurt and embarrassed, but I didn't say anything. As she railed on, several of the white kids glanced over at me and rolled their eyes. I sensed they were saying what I was thinking: "What a dummy she is!"

The third incident came when Curtis and I decided to play football. We weren't big, but we were fast, so we could outrun everyone else. Apparently, our performance on the field upset some of the white people who watched our practices because a few of them surrounded us one day as Curtis and I walked off the field.

"If you guys come back here, we're going to throw you in the river," one of them said in a menacing tone. Then they walked away.

I don't know if they really would have done that, but Curtis and I decided we had better things to do than play football.

I never told Mother about these incidents because I know it would have hurt her. Just as she protected us from the hurtful truth about our dad, now it was my turn to protect her.

CHAPTER 5

Trying to Fit In

Halfway through my eighth grade year, we moved back to our old house—the one we lived in before the divorce. Mother's hard work and frugality allowed her to regain the house, but it required a change in schools. Curtis went to Southwestern High while I enrolled at Hunter Junior High, a predominately black school. I hated leaving Wilson but loved moving back into our little house, which seemed like a mansion to me.

I'm not sure if it was adolescence or the insecurity of being the new kid, but the move introduced me to something I'd never experienced before: the constant temptation to become one of the guys. It started with a rather disrespectful practice known as capping, and it went like this.

"Know what the Indians did with General Custer's worn-out clothes?" one of the guys asked in my presence.

"Tell us," someone shot back.

"They saved them, and now our man Carson wears them!"

Of course, everyone laughed as I felt the heat rising up my neck and cheeks.

They kept at it for weeks until I finally realized the best way to beat them was to join them. So the next time one of the guys tried to make me the object of his capping, I took over.

"Man, Carson, that shirt you're wearing has been through World War I, World War II, and World War III."

"Yeah," I retorted, "and your mama wore it!"

From that point on, the in-crowd stopped tormenting me as I out-capped the top cappers throughout the whole school. It felt great to finally be one of the guys, but I learned quickly that trying to fit in is a never-ending—and expensive— game. By the time I was in ninth grade, I realized my clothes weren't good enough. One day I came home and announced to Mother that I needed new pants. "I can't wear these anymore, Mother. Everyone laughs at them"

"Only stupid people laugh at what you wear, Bennie," she said. "It's not what you wear that makes the difference."

And it wasn't just the pants. The popular guys wore Italian knit shirts, alligator shoes, and leather jackets, and I wanted to be just like them. So every day I begged and pressured my mother, insensitive to the reality that although she worked hard, she had little money to spare. All I cared about was fitting in.

Finally, Mother relented. "If having new clothes will make you happy, I'll try to buy some of those fancy clothes for you."

And she did. But that wasn't enough. I started hanging out after school, coming in late, and ignoring my homework. My grades started to drop, but I didn't care. The cool guys invited me to their parties and jam sessions. I was having fun—more than I'd ever had in my life—because I was now one of the cool guys.

I just wasn't very happy.

I had strayed from the important and basic values that came from my mother's deep faith in God. Mother first learned about Jesus Christ when she was in the hospital to deliver me. A woman named Mary Thomas visited her and began talking about God. Then, when Mother struggled with depression, that same woman showed up and invited Mother to accept Jesus as her Savior.

"There's another source of strength, Sonya, and this strength can be yours."

Mother began attending the Sharon Seventh-day Adventist Church in Inkster, a suburb of Detroit. Though she only had a third-grade education and could barely read, she taught herself to read well by reading the Bible every day. Of course she took Curtis and me to church with her, so we both knew how God wanted us to live. I even asked the pastor to rebaptize me because I thought I'd come to a better understanding of what it meant to be a Christian.

But deep inside, I was still more interested in fitting in and having a good time, which blinded me to a problem that almost ruined my life forever.

CHAPTER 6

The Fire Inside

We were walking out of English class when Jerry taunted me. "That sure was a dumb thing to say." He said it loud enough that kids crowded around us, hoping for a little action.

"I guess so," I shrugged.

"You guess?" Jerry roared. "Listen, Carson, that was one of the all-time stupid things of the year!"

Feeling my temperature rise, I took the bait.

"You've said some pretty dumb things too," I retorted.

"Oh yeah?"

"Yeah, just last week you ..."

By now, more kids crowded around us as our words flew back and forth. I tried to remain calm as Jerry's voice grew louder and louder. Finally I turned to my locker, thinking if I just ignored him, he would go away. My fingers spun the dial on my combination lock, and when it opened, I pulled it from the latch. That's when Jerry shoved me. In an instant I swung at him with the lock in my hand, slamming it into his forehead. He staggered backward, groaned, then lifted his hand to his forehead. When he felt the sticky blood on his fingers and lowered his hand in front of his eyes, he screamed.

Later, in the principal's office, I apologized to Jerry, and the incident was closed. But then a few weeks later, my temper reared its ugly head in a much more disturbing way. Mother had brought home a new pair of pants for me, and I refused to wear them. They weren't the style that all the other guys were wearing, so I told her to take them back.

"I can't take them back, Bennie. They were on sale."

"I don't care," I yelled as I spun around to face her. "I hate them and wouldn't be caught dead in them! They're not what I want."

She took a step toward me and said, "Bennie, we don't always get what we want in life."

As I screamed at Mother, telling her that *I* was going to get everything I wanted out of life, I raised my right arm and swung toward my mother. Thankfully, Curtis grabbed me from behind and wrestled me away. Otherwise, I would have hit my own mother. That should have been a wakeup call, but I didn't want to face the truth about myself: I might have been a pretty good kid, but I had a terrible temper. Once I reached the boiling point, I lost control, usually grabbing the first thing I could find to bash someone.

It all crashed down in the ninth grade when my friend and I were listening to a transistor radio. He switched stations, making fun of the music I was listening to. That set me off.

"It's better than anything you like," I yelled, grabbing for the radio.

"Come on, Carson. You always ..."

And that's when I reached for the camping knife I carried in my back pocket. Flipping the blade open, I lunged for his belly. Instead of stabbing him, the knife hit his big ROTC belt buckle and snapped. Had he not been wearing that belt, Bob would be lying at my feet, dying or severely wounded. I was numb, unbelieving. I muttered an apology and ran home, heading straight for the bathroom.

No one was home as I sat on the linoleum floor, filled with shame and guilt. Here I was at age fourteen with dreams of becoming a doctor, but I couldn't control my temper. I hated myself but couldn't help myself, so I hated myself even more. By then I'd begun reading *Psychology Today*, and it dawned on me that my temper could be a personality disorder that might be impossible to fix. I sat on the floor of the bathroom for more than two hours, filled with remorse and a sense of helplessness, until I recalled something my mother had taught me: when you need help, pray.

So I begged God to take away my anger.

"If you don't do this for me, God, I have no place else to go."

I slipped out of the bathroom, grabbed a Bible, and began reading Proverbs: "He who is slow to anger is better than the mighty, and he who rules his spirit than he who takes a city" (Proverbs 16:32 RSV). While those words condemned me, they also gave me hope, and soon I began to feel a sense of peace sweep over me.

God heard my prayer that day. I walked out of the bathroom a changed young man. Since that day, I have never had a problem with my temper. I can tolerate amazing amounts of stress and ridicule as God has helped me conquer my terrible temper once and for all. The One who created the universe can do anything, and I have the evidence—my own experience. He changed me, and since that day when I was fourteen, I began to focus on the future. My mother's lessons—and those of several of my teachers—were at last starting to pay off.

CHAPTER 7

High School Heroes

Every kid should have a big brother like Curtis. Unlike me, Curtis never got caught up in the peer thing. He stayed on the honor roll all through high school, then went on to the University of Michigan, where he majored in engineering. His influence on me was enormous.

For example, when I was thirteen I decided I wanted to become a psychiatrist. So what would any big brother do when he learned of his little brother's interest? He gave me a subscription to *Psychology Today*. He was only fifteen and earned a little spending money at his after-school job in the science lab, so that was a big sacrifice on his part. But that was Curtis—generous and sensitive to my needs.

Then in the second half of my sophomore year of high school, I joined the ROTC, largely because of Curtis. I really admired him, and it made me so proud to see him in uniform with more medals and ribbons on his chest than anyone else. I wanted to be just like him, so I joined, and my ROTC experience helped me get back on track. For one thing, it got me out of caring so much about my clothes— three days a week I had to wear the ROTC uniform. But it also gave me—along with a lot of other people—the confidence I needed to excel.

One of those people was a student named Sharper who had reached the highest achievable ROTC rank—full colonel. Sharper seemed so mature, so self-assured, and yet likeable. I thought, *If Sharper can make colonel, why can't I?* Even though I had gotten a late start and was a semester behind everyone else in my class, I made that my goal.

Teachers also played an important role in my transition from slacker to achiever. They gave me personal attention, encouraged me, and inspired me to keep trying my hardest. Mrs. Miller, my ninth-grade English teacher, took a special interest in me, often spending extra time with me after class. She taught me to appreciate good literature and poetry and would go over my papers until I corrected every mistake. When my grades started to drop in the tenth grade, even though she was no longer my teacher, she kept after me. I hated disappointing her.

Then there was Frank McCotter, my biology teacher. He had so much confidence in me—more than I had in myself. He pushed me by having me design experiments for the other students, set them up, and keep the lab running smoothly. Lemuel Doakes, who directed the band, demanded perfection from all of us. But he was more than a music teacher. Even though he saw that I had musical talent, he pulled me aside and said, "Carson, put academics first. Always put first things first."

Of course, undergirding all this support was Mother. Despite my lack of interest in school, she never lectured me. Instead, she memorized poems and famous sayings and kept quoting them to me. Despite her limited education, she could quote entire poems, like Robert Frost's "The Road Not Taken." She often quoted another poem by a woman named Mayme White Miller. It was called "You Have Yourself to Blame," and that message finally began to sink in. I realized that the in-group had no power over me. I could choose to wear whatever clothes I wanted and to take school seriously even if they didn't.

With all that help, how could I not succeed? But what really kept me focused on success was the ROTC. I earned a lot of medals and won just about every competition they offered, and along with all of this I got promoted rapidly. When I was a master sergeant, for example, Sergeant Bandy, an instructor in the United States Army and the head of our high school unit, put me in charge of the fifth-hour ROTC unit. They were so rambunctious that none of the other student sergeants could handle them, but he offered me a little incentive. If I could turn things around with them, he'd promote me to second lieutenant—unheard of for someone of my rank.

That was all I needed. I got to know the guys, and when I discovered they loved fancy drill routines, I offered extra practice if they behaved during the regular teaching session. I also borrowed from my past experience in capping. They soon learned I could make them look pretty foolish if they got out of line. Maybe not the best method, but it worked.

At the end of the semester, Sergeant Bandy called me into his office and said, "Carson, the fifth-hour class is the best unit in the school. I'm promoting you to second lieutenant."

That promotion opened the door to my real goal, which was to make full colonel. The normal progression went from second lieutenant to first lieutenant to captain to major. After that, if you were lucky, you went on to become lieutenant colonel. Only three students in the entire city of Detroit made it to full colonel, and that intensified my desire to make the grade.

About that time, Sergeant Bandy was replaced by Sergeant Hunt, the first black sergeant in charge of our ROTC unit. Like so many of the adults at the high school, he took a special interest in me, often pulling me aside and barking things like, "Carson, you gotta learn this, and you gotta learn it perfect."

When I went for my field-grade examination, along with students from each of the twenty-two schools in the city, I made the highest score—the highest any student had ever received. To my surprise, they promoted me from second lieutenant all the way to lieutenant colonel. I could hardly believe it. Beginning in the second half of tenth grade, I had gone from private to lieutenant colonel by the time I reached the twelfth grade. With a full semester of school left, I actually had a chance to become colonel. After a lot more study, I sat for the exam and again scored the highest among all the competitors. Not only did I make full colonel, but they made me city executive officer over all the other schools.

All because I wanted to be like Curtis.

I was so proud to lead the Memorial Day parade, a heavy cluster of medals and braids on my chest. I got to meet two Vietnam War veterans who had won the Congressional Medal of Honor, as well as Gen. William Westmoreland. Later, I was offered a scholarship to West Point, which I eventually turned down. It flattered me, though, and proved that Mother was right all along when she constantly told me I could do anything I set my mind to.

It was one thing, however, to excel at an inner-city, mostly black high school. Did I have what it takes to make it in college?

CHAPTER 8

You're Not in High School
Anymore

My hard work paid off. Dozens of colleges offered me scholarships, but I narrowed my choices to Yale and Harvard. One of my favorite television programs was *College Bowl,* a quiz show that pitted college academic teams against each other. Shortly before I had to make up my mind, Harvard and Yale went at it on *College Bowl,* and Yale crushed Harvard, something like 520–35. So of course I chose Yale.

I strode onto campus feeling pretty smug about my accomplishments, and the luxurious student housing added to what can only be described as pride. The tall gothic buildings, ivy-covered walls, and tree-lined walkways seemed appropriate for a kid with high SAT scores, a brilliant academic record, and long list of achievements in the ROTC. Until I soon realized that every other student was just as bright, if not smarter.

Yale was a great leveler for me.

Not only were my SAT scores lower than many of my peers', but my dream of becoming a doctor faced an insurmountable hurdle: chemistry. You see, I never really learned how to study in high school, usually waiting until the day before a test to cram. Since I memorized things easily, I aced all my tests. That didn't work in my chemistry class at Yale—my grades quickly dropped, and along with them, my confidence. I was failing chemistry and failing it badly. And if I failed chemistry, I couldn't stay in the premed program. My only hope was a policy the professor offered. If a failing student did well on the final exam, he would throw out most of the bad grades and allow you to pass the course. But since I squandered away the entire course, passing the final—let alone scoring well—was out of the question. My dream of becoming a doctor was about to end badly, but for some reason I just accepted it.

What am I doing at Yale anyway? Who do I think I am? Just a dumb black kid from the poor side of Detroit who has no business trying to make it through Yale with all its intelligent, affluent students.

It's amazing how easily we can believe a lie. I pretty much caved in to the idea that I would never become a doctor. The night before the final exam I sat in my room listening to the wind rustling through the trees outside my window. A tall, skinny kid with his head in his hands, I was finally facing a challenge I couldn't overcome. I had failed. But then in the back of my mind I heard Mother's stern but reassuring voice: "Bennie, you can do it! I believe in you!"

Recalling the many times she told me to pray whenever anything seemed too difficult, I reached out to God: "Either help me understand what other career you have for me, or perform a miracle and help me pass my final exam."

It was late—around 10:00 p.m. I was tired. But I had to try. For the next two hours, I poured over formulas that had no meaning to me. I scribbled terms on a sheet of paper. I poured over the material I should have been studying regularly throughout the semester. Only this time, cramming wasn't working. This was Yale, not Southwestern High School.

I flopped onto my bed and whispered a prayer: "God, I'm sorry. Please forgive me for failing you and for failing myself." Then I fell asleep.

To this day, I believe God responded to my prayer with a dream. In that dream, a man walked into a room, stopped at the chalkboard, and started working out chemistry problems. When I awoke, I recalled most of the problems he had worked out in my dream. The ones I couldn't remember, I looked up in my textbook. I dressed, ate breakfast, then hurried off to my exam, only to discover that the questions in my test booklet mirrored the ones from my dream. I almost laughed as my pencil flew through the solutions. As I turned in my test, I knew I had passed and thanked God for pulling off a miracle, adding: "I promise to never put you in that situation again."

That's also when I realized with certainty that God not only wanted me to be a doctor, but he also had special tasks for me to do. I started learning how to study rather than merely passing exams. In every class I aimed to grasp every little detail. God had done his part, and now it was my turn to prepare myself for the future.

A few days later, the chemistry grades were posted, and there it was: "Benjamin S. Carson—97." Right back up there with the best in the class.

CHAPTER 9

More Than a Job

Despite earning a scholarship to Yale, I needed a
job to pay for things like clothes, books, transportation, and dozens of other expenses I knew I'd
face. Perhaps because of Mother's example, I never
shied away from hard work, having worked all
through high school in the school laboratory and in
neighboring Wayne State University's biology lab.
But as my high school graduation approached and I
hadn't found anything, I was desperate.

One of my counselors, Alma Whittley, knew of
my need and called an acquaintance at the Ford
Motor Company.

"We've got a young fellow here named Ben
Carson who's very bright and going to Yale in September. He needs a job, right now!"

It worked. The day after high school graduation
I reported to Ford's main administration building
in Dearborn, where I was assigned to the payroll
department. I considered it a prestigious job, or,
as my mother called it, "the big time," because I
had to wear a white shirt and tie every day. I might
have gotten that job from someone else's influence,
but that wasn't enough to keep it. Nor was knowing a lot of information, though that helps. What I
learned from this job is that it's not who you know
or what you know, but the quality of your work

that makes a difference. That summer I determined that no matter what the job, I would work to be the best person they ever hired.

The summer after my first year at Yale, I got a great job supervising a highway work crew. A federally funded program provided work for inner-city students. Every day we would walk along the interstate near Detroit and the western suburbs, picking up and bagging trash. Most of the other supervisors had a horrible time keeping the kids focused. Unaccustomed to hard work, they complained about the heat, the pay, and just about everything else. The average amount of trash picked up each day amounted to a measly ten to twelve bags. I may be an overachiever, but I thought that was ridiculous. So after the third or fourth day I came up with a little out-of-the-box method to increase productivity.

"From now on, everyone shows up for work at six in the morning," I announced to a chorus of objections.

The normal workday was 7:30 a.m. until 4:30 p.m., but I made a deal with them. If they got to work at six when it was still cool out and worked real fast, as soon as they filled 150 bags they were done for the day. Already, this crew had approached 100 bags a day and loved bragging to the other crews about their productivity. So after batting the idea around, they agreed.

The next day they showed up at 6:00 a.m. sharp and worked harder and faster than ever. After about three hours, they had their 150 bags.

"Okay, guys," I announced after counting the last bag. "You're done for the day!"

They were ecstatic and, from that point on, worked with a joyful playfulness. Sometimes we would return to the Department of Transportation with our work done just as the other crews were getting started.

"You guys working today?" one of my guys would laughingly shout.

"Man, not much trash to pick up today after Superman and his hotshots picked it all up already."

Of course, the other supervisors knew what was going on but kept quiet about it. I'm sure that if the higher-ups had a serious problem with the way I motivated my crew, they would have told me to stop. But I've always believed that if you can find a better way to do something, just go ahead and do it, as long as it's reasonable and doesn't hurt anyone.

During my time at Yale, I always managed to find work during the summer, even during the summer of 1971 when the economy slid into a slump. In addition to the Department of Transportation, I worked in the mailroom at an advertising company and on the assembly line at Chrysler. Still, I never seemed to have enough money to make it through an entire school year. Looking back, I can see that God used my lack of money to show me that he would always take care of me.

For example, toward the end of my sophomore year, I received notice that all the final exams in my psychology class had been accidentally burned in the trash. We would have to repeat the test. So I, along with 150 other students, returned to the designated auditorium where our test awaited us. Only it was a markedly different test. The questions were incredibly difficult, if not impossible to answer based on the lectures and reading assignments.

"Forget it," I heard one girl say to another. "Let's go back and study this. We can just say we didn't read the notice. Then when they give us the test, we'll be ready." The two left the auditorium. Immediately, three others packed up and left. Within ten minutes, half the class had left, and within a half hour, I was the only student left. Like the others, I was tempted to walk out, but I had read the notice and couldn't lie and say that I hadn't. I just decided to do my best and pray to God to help me figure out what to write.

Suddenly, the auditorium door opened noisily. It was the professor, with a photographer from the Yale *Daily News* in tow.

"What's going on?" I asked.

"A hoax," the professor smiled. "We wanted to see who was the most honest student in class. And that's you. Here."

As the photographer snapped my picture, she handed me a ten-dollar bill. Clearly a gift from God, but I was about to receive an even better one.

CHAPTER 10

"I Guess I Like You"

As I approached my third year at Yale, the last thing on my mind was love. I wasn't about to let a relationship get in the way of my plans to become a doctor. That, plus my somewhat shy personality and lack of money essentially took dating off the table, which was absolutely fine with me.

And then I met Candy.

That summer Yale hosted a reception for new students at the posh Grosse Pointe Country Club. The admissions office asked me to attend with a few other local upperclassmen to welcome the incoming freshmen from Michigan. As I mingled among the guests, I couldn't help but notice the good-looking girl with an outgoing nature and easy laugh.

"I've always been called Candy," she introduced herself, "but my name is Lacena Rustin."

Just talking with her made me feel good. Her hair fluffed around her face in the popular Afro, and her smile could melt an ice floe. But what drew me to her most was her effervescent personality. I admired her from the start, and once the semester began, I checked in with her now and then—you know, just to make sure she was adjusting to college life.

It turns out that she was doing just fine. In addition to getting straight A's, she played violin in the

Yale Symphony and Bach Society—both of which admitted only top-flight musicians. Since one of my mentors in Detroit had gotten me interested in classical music, this gave us something to talk about whenever Candy and I would pass from time to time on campus. I tried to convince myself that while she was certainly special, Candy Rustin was just another student.

Although she wasn't particularly religious, she accepted my invitation to attend church in New Haven, and when she learned that I sang in the choir, she joined too. The rest of the choir appreciated the addition of a lovely alto voice, and it wasn't long before she was a regular at Mount Zion. She even began attending Bible classes. Later, she explained to me that she had always had a hunger for God, but what attracted her to Mount Zion was the people.

"They loved me into the faith."

Her family thought it was strange that she went to church on a Saturday, but I guess they approved. Her mother soon became an active Adventist herself. And I was becoming more interested in Candy.

By my senior year, we were spending a lot of time together. Just before Thanksgiving, the admissions office asked us to do some recruiting in Detroit-area high schools, providing a modest expense account that allowed me to rent a little Ford Pinto and take Candy to a couple of nice restaurants. We had a wonderful time, and I slowly began to realize that I liked Candy a lot. More than I'd been aware of, more than I'd ever liked any girl.

We stayed a little longer than I'd planned because I wanted Candy to meet my mother and some of my friends. So to get the Pinto back on time, we had to drive straight through to New Haven from Detroit. A light snow had fallen as I eased the car onto the interstate, and by the time we crossed into Ohio, Candy had drifted off to sleep. There wasn't much traffic, so to make good time I pushed the Pinto well over the 70-mile-per-hour speed limit. Nearing Youngstown, the monotony of the nearly straight highway and warmth of the heater soon took effect. I floated off into a comfortable sleep, only to be awakened to the jarring sound of my tires hitting those reflectors that divide the highway's lanes. My headlights pierced the blackness of a deep ravine as I quickly hit the brakes and jerked the steering wheel to the left to avoid flying over the edge. That sent the Pinto into a full 360, screeching to a halt next to the shoulder. With hands shaking, I eased the car onto the gravel shoulder just as an 18-wheeler barreled through the lane I had just vacated.

It all happened in a few seconds, yet in that brief time, I fully concentrated on being ready to die. I turned off the ignition, and as my heart raced I kept repeating, "I'm alive. Thank you, God. I'm alive!"

Candy slept through the whole thing but awoke when I shut off the engine.

"What's going on?" she asked.

I didn't want to scare her, so I told her everything was fine and that I just took a quick rest.

"Everything can't be fine if we're not moving and the engine's not running. Ben, please tell me what's wrong."

When I told her what really happened, she reached across the darkness and put her hand in mine. "Ben, the Lord spared our lives. He's got plans for us."

Neither of us slept again that night, talking the whole time about everything under the sun. At one point, she asked me why I was so nice to her.

"I just like being nice to second-year Yale students," I joked.

"Ben, be serious."

As the first rays of light appeared on the horizon, I felt something inside that I'd never felt before. "I guess it's because I like you," I finally offered. "I guess I like you a lot."

"I like you too, Ben. More than anybody I've ever met."

I eased the car off the road until it stopped. Then I reached over and put my arm around Candy and kissed her. Somehow I knew she'd kiss me back, and she did—our first kiss. Neither of us knew much about romance, but we both understood one thing—we loved each other.

CHAPTER 11

Discovering a Gift

To become a doctor after four years of under-graduate studies, you need to get accepted into medical school and then spend four more years of intensive training. If you don't get into a medical school, then your hopes of becoming a doctor are over, and that created a lot of stress for my premed classmates. As one of my classmates said several times, "If I don't make it into med school, I've just been wasting all this time."

I never worried much about it, and it must have shown because one day one of my friends asked me, "Carson, why aren't you freaking out like the rest of us?"

"Because I know I'm getting into the University of Michigan Medical School."

"Oh, really? How can you be so sure?"

"It's simple; my father owns the university."

I was teasing, knowing that a lot of students came from wealthy families who could pull strings. It was kind of funny overhearing a conversation in which someone said, "Carson's old man owns the University of Michigan." But as a Christian, I believed that God—my heavenly Father—created the universe and owns everything in it, including the University of Michigan.

I finally graduated from Yale in 1973 with a fairly respectable grade-point average, although far from the top of my class. But I was satisfied because I knew I had given it my all. As it turned out, I did get accepted to Michigan, which was great because not only was it in my home state, which meant my tuition would be lower, but it was one of the top medical schools in the nation. Candy still had two years before finishing at Yale, and we were so much in love that we wrote each other every single day. We still have those boxes of letters.

Occasionally, when I had a little extra money, I would call her—that was before cell phones, when "long distance" rates encouraged brief conversations. But one time we must have been especially lonely because we talked for six hours! The next day I began worrying about the bill—whatever it was, I wouldn't be able to pay it. But for some reason, the call never showed up on my phone bill. I surmised that some billing clerk saw the call and decided no one could talk that long on the phone.

Even with the lower in-state tuition, I still needed to work during the summer before starting at Michigan, and once again I faced a stagnant job market. Detroit businesses weren't hiring—they were laying off people. At the time, Mother cared for the children of the Sennet family, and Mr. Sennet owned a steel company. So naturally, Mother told Mr. Sennet that her son needed a job, and he hired me.

When I showed up for work, the foreman turned me into a crane operator, an extremely responsible—and difficult—job. To operate the crane, you had to have an understanding of physics to move the boom over and down to the steel. After showing me the ropes, I climbed up into the cab of a giant crane and, by manipulating the controls with both hands, lifted stacks of steel that weighed several tons, swinging them carefully over to the waiting trucks, then lowering them gently onto the truck beds. There wasn't much space to maneuver, and one wrong move could spell disaster. Not exactly the kind of work for an aspiring physician. Or was it?

Operating that crane all summer made me aware that I possess an unusual ability—a divine gift, I believe—of extraordinary eye-hand coordination. I believe that God gives all of us gifts that we have the privilege of developing so that we can serve him and others. Some are given the gift of teaching or preaching. Some the gift of hospitality. Or, as with Candy, the gift of music. Although I didn't know my specialty at the time, God must have, for eye-hand coordination is essential for a surgeon.

One aspect of this gift is the ability to "see" in three dimensions. It's just something I am able to do without even thinking about it. Seeing in three dimensions seems incredibly simple, but many doctors don't naturally have this ability. And if they don't learn it, they just don't develop into outstanding surgeons and frequently encounter problems in the operating room.

I probably shouldn't admit it, but this gift came in handy while I was an undergrad at Yale and needed a break from my studies. One of my friends introduced me to the game of foosball (sometimes called table soccer). I had never played it before, but I immediately picked it up as if I was a veteran foosballer. I was able to see the entire table and knew which handle to spin as my opponents frequently reached for the wrong one. When I returned to Yale in 1988, I ran into an old classmate who is now on the staff at the university. He laughingly told me that I was so good at foosball that after I left, they named several plays "Carson shots."

I don't take my eye-hand coordination for granted. It is a gift from God. In fact, it's the most valuable talent God has given me and the reason people sometimes say I have gifted hands.

CHAPTER 12

Hooked on the Brain

Ever since I got my first pair of glasses and realized I could learn with the best of them, I've wanted to know more. It's almost become a compulsion: *I have to know more.* Which was how I discovered my first innovation in brain surgery. I was in my clinical year at Michigan, on my neurosurgery rotation. Each rotation lasted a month, and on this particular occasion I observed my instructor trying to locate the foramen ovale—the hole at the base of the skull. He was having obvious difficulty finding it as he probed into the patient's skull with a long, thin needle.

"There's got to be an easier way to do this," I thought. Having to probe around wasted precious surgery time and didn't help the patient much either. I contacted some friends I'd made in the radiology department when I worked there one summer, and they let me experiment with their equipment. I eventually found that by placing two tiny metal rings on the back and front of the skull and passing an x-ray beam through them, I could easily locate the foramen ovale. When I tried it in actual surgery, it worked. The professor observing me shook his head and smiled, "That's fabulous, Carson."

During my second rotation—my fourth year of medical school—it became clear that I knew more about neurosurgery than the interns and junior resident. Despite the fact that I was still only a student, they often handed me their beepers and headed off to catch some sleep—always with the expectation that if I got into something I couldn't handle, I could call them. Talk about an emotional high. I had worked so hard and pursued an in-depth knowledge of neurosurgery, and it was paying off. If I was going to be a surgeon, I wanted to be the best, most-informed surgeon I could possibly be.

I'll never forget the first times I looked down upon a human brain and saw human hands working on that center of intelligence, emotion, and motion. Hands that were working to heal. I was hooked. I knew I had found my calling.

All the facets of my career came together then. My interest in neurosurgery, my growing interest in the study of the brain, and the acceptance of my God-given talent of eye-hand coordination. Neurosurgery seemed the most natural thing in the world to me.

When it came time for my own internship and residency, I would have stayed at Michigan. But the department was going through some changes, so I applied to Johns Hopkins University. Despite my good grades and high scores on national board examinations, getting accepted was anything but a slam dunk. Johns Hopkins accepted only two students a year for neurosurgeon residencies. On average, 125 applied.

Within weeks of applying, I was invited for an interview, one of only a few granted. Thanks to one of my mentors in Detroit, the one who had earlier introduced me to classical music, my interview with Dr. George Udvarhelyi went extremely well. I think we talked more about classical music than medicine. Soon I received word that I had been accepted into the neurosurgery program at Johns Hopkins, and I entered a rigorous program with a confidence born of a good mother, hard work, and trust in God. Whenever I faced a challenge, I recalled Mother's words: "Bennie, you can do anything."

If my professional life was moving beautifully, my personal life was even better. Candy graduated from Yale in the spring of 1975, and we got married on July 6. After I finished medical school, we moved to Baltimore, where Candy not only worked several jobs to support us, but earned her master's degree in business. Both of us were living out a belief that I have to this day. In any career, whether as a surgeon, a musician, or a secretary, one needs to have a confidence that says, "I can do anything, and if I can't do it, I know how to get help."

At this time I also learned to pay attention to "the common people." The nurses, clerks, and aides who are a vital part of the team that helps heal patients. Unfortunately, I saw too many doctors treat these dedicated employees poorly. I went out of my way to get to know these people because they often had insights into a patient's wellbeing that doctors missed.

Today, I try to emphasize this when I speak to young people: "There isn't anybody in the world who isn't worth something. Every person you meet is one of God's children." I truly believe that being a successful neurosurgeon doesn't make me better than anyone else. It means that I'm fortunate because God gave me the talent to do this job well. I also believe that whatever talents I have, I need to share them with others.

CHAPTER 13

Hitting My Stride

Even in the 1970s at a prestigious institution like Johns Hopkins, people were not accustomed to seeing a black doctor. Sometimes it was almost humorous; other times, more disturbing. More than once, nurses thought I was an orderly or physical therapist—anything but a doctor. Even though I always tried to be polite when that happened, the nurses couldn't hide their embarrassment: "New intern? But you can't—I mean—I didn't mean to …" I honestly felt sorry for them because they likely had never encountered a black intern before.

Then there were the patients who didn't want a black doctor caring for them. When they complained to the head of neurosurgery, Dr. Donlin Long, he always answered in a calm but firm voice: "There's the door. You're welcome to go, but if you stay, Dr. Carson will handle your case." This all happened behind my back; Dr. Long only told me about these incidents much later.

I really didn't worry about the occasional prejudice I faced. My bigger concern was to be a role model for black youth. I want them to see that the only way out of their often dismal situations is contained within themselves. I believe that many of our pressing racial problems will be taken care of when we minorities stand on our own two feet and refuse to expect others to rescue us. We need to be self-reliant, not self-centered, which means demanding the best of ourselves while extending a hand to others.

...

After completing my internship, I was invited by Dr. Long to stay at Johns Hopkins for my residency in neurosurgery, bypassing a required two-year stint in general surgery. During this period, I was also a senior resident at Baltimore City Hospital (now Francis Scott Key Medical Center). The two hospitals prepared me in ways I could never have imagined.

For example, one night paramedics brought a comatose patient to Baltimore City. He had been beaten with a baseball bat, and his condition was deteriorating rapidly. I knew that without a lobectomy (removing the frontal lobe of the brain), the patient would die, but I couldn't locate a faculty member or attending surgeon. I had two choices: perform the lobectomy myself, which violated hospital policy, or let the man die.

The physician's assistant, Ed Rosenquist, knew what I was going through and uttered three words: "Go for it." Once I made the decision, a calmness came over me. The surgery went like clockwork, and the man woke up a few hours later, perfectly normal neurologically. Had things turned out differently, I might have been censured.

One of the highlights of my residency was the research I conducted during my fifth year. I had become interested in brain tumors and neuro-oncology. Up to that point, researchers had had little luck growing tumors in small animals. Mice were too small. Monkeys too expensive. I asked a lot of questions and landed on using New Zealand white rabbits, benefitting largely from Dr. Jim Anderson who worked with liver and kidney tumors. With his help, we used something he called VX-2 to implant tumors in the rabbits' brains, and to our surprise, the tumors grew. But that was only half the battle.

Working closely with biochemist Dr. John Hilton, we used a combination of enzymes to dissolve the connected tissue, leaving the cancer cells intact, and we soon had the necessary ingredient of viability—almost 100 percent of the cells survived. From there we concentrated the cells in the quantities we wanted, resulting in the kind of consistency that allows researchers to learn how brain tumors grow.

Normally this kind of research would have taken years to accomplish, but because I had so much collaboration with others at Hopkins helping me iron out the problems, the research model was completed in six months. Not only did I win the Resident of the Year Award for this research, I went right into my chief residency instead of staying in the lab for two years.

I entered that chief residency with a quiet excitement. I was ready to get my hands on surgical instruments and learn how to perform delicate procedures in a quick, efficient way. I learned how to remove brain tumors and how to clip aneurysms. I learned how to correct malformations of bone and tissue and to operate on the spine. I learned how to use an air-powered drill to cut through bone only millimeters away from nerves and brain tissue. I learned the special skills that transformed the instruments along with my hands, eyes, and intuition into healing.

I finished my residency ready to move on. A life-changing event lay ahead of me, though I didn't know it. It appeared as an impossible idea—at first.

CHAPTER 14

A Dream Come True

As Candy and I buckled ourselves in for the long flight to Australia, I wondered if I'd made the right decision. At the urging of Bryant Stokes, a senior neurosurgeon at Johns Hopkins who was from Perth, I agreed to a year as senior registrar—sort of a cross between a chief resident and junior faculty member—at Sir Charles Gardiner Hospital of Queen Elizabeth II Medical Center. It was the major teaching center in Western Australia, and their only referral center for neurosurgery.

Although Australia had abolished their "whites-only" laws in 1968, I wondered how people there would react to a black physician. When my friends heard I was considering moving to the other side of the planet, they doggedly tried to talk me out of it.

"You'll be back in a week," one well-intentioned friend said.

Then there was my concern for Candy. While I was chief resident at Johns Hopkins, she became pregnant with twins, but miscarried in her fifth month. Pregnant again, her doctor put her on bed rest after the fourth month. Maybe this wasn't the best time to be moving to Australia, a question shared by her friends.

"They do have qualified doctors in Australia," she said firmly, but with a smile.

Almost from the time the 747's wheels touched the runway in Perth, my fears vanished. The Australians received us warmly, and our being affiliated with the Seventh-day Adventist Church opened many doors. On our first Saturday in Australia, the pastor announced to the congregation, "We have a family from the United States with us today. They're going to be here for a year." He then introduced Candy and me and encouraged everyone to greet us.

Did they ever! After the service, everyone crowded around us. Seeing that Candy was pregnant, they asked us what we needed. Because we were limited in the amount of luggage we could carry, over the next few days those wonderful people brought us bassinets, blankets, baby strollers, and diapers—or what they called nappies. We also received countless invitations to dinner.

One day, Candy and I were having dinner with some new friends from the hospital, and one of the residents asked, "How do you know so many people?"

"We come from a large family," I responded.

"You mean you have relatives here in Australia?" he asked incredulously.

"Sort of," I laughed and then explained that in the church, we think of ourselves as belonging to God's family.

He'd never heard of such a concept.

Being the senior registrar, I got to do most of the cases, which boosted my appreciation for being in "the land down under." And Candy jumped right in as well, landing the positions of first violinist with the local symphony and vocalist in a professional ensemble. Within a month, I faced my first real challenge in the operating room.

The senior consultant—the top person in an Australian hospital—diagnosed a young woman as having an acoustic neuroma, a tumor that grows at the base of the skull and causes deafness and weakness of the facial muscles. The tumor was so large that the consultant had to tell the woman that in removing it, he wouldn't be able to save any of her cranial nerves.

Privately, I asked the senior consultant if I could try removing the tumor using a microscopic technique. "If it works," I told him, "I think I can possibly save the nerves."

He told me to go ahead and give it a try, but I could tell from his tone that he was annoyed at my youthful confidence. The surgery took ten hours, without rest, but despite my fatigue, I was elated. I had completely removed the tumor *and* saved the cranial nerves. The young woman enjoyed a complete recovery, eventually becoming pregnant and naming her baby after the senior consultant who she thought had performed the surgery. That was okay with me because I had earned his respect. Word spread quickly, and soon he and the other senior consultants would approach me and ask, "Carson, can you cover a surgery for me?"

It soon became clear that God had led me to Australia to give me unheard of experience in brain surgery. I became the local expert in the field. I did a lot of tough cases, some absolutely spectacular. Where else would I have gotten such a unique opportunity for volume surgery immediately after my residency? Even better, while we were there, Candy gave birth to our first child, Murray.

Upon returning to Johns Hopkins, I got another surprise. The chief of pediatric neurosurgery left, and Dr. Long proposed to the board that I assume the position. When he informed me that the board accepted his recommendation, I was deeply grateful and humbled. At thirty-three, I became the chief pediatric neurosurgeon at Johns Hopkins.

Within a year I faced one of the most challenging surgeries of my life. The little girl's name was Maranda, and she would have a tremendous influence on my career. And my choice of a surgical procedure would attract more attention than I would have liked.

CHAPTER 15

Holding Life or Death in
My Hands

The Franciscos—Luis and Terry—had run out of options. Their daughter, Maranda, suffered from a rare disease known as Rasmussen's encephalitis. Now four years old, Maranda had suffered debilitating seizures since she was eighteen months. By the time they reached out to us at Johns Hopkins, she was experiencing up to a hundred seizures a day, as often as three minutes apart. The danger of choking was so great that she had to be fed through a tube; the seizures also caused her to forget how to walk, talk, and learn.

Luis and Terry took her from specialist to specialist, yet none were able to do much more than prescribe various medications—thirty-five different drugs in all. Despite the impact on their modest income, they never gave up trying to find someone who could help their daughter. "If there is any place on earth to get help for Maranda, we're going to find it," they once told a reporter.

But time was running out. The disease progressively leads to permanent paralysis on one side of the body, mental retardation, and then death.

After reviewing Maranda's extensive medical records and CT scans, one of my colleagues, Dr. John Freeman, concluded that her only hope lay in a controversial procedure known as a hemispherec-tomy—literally removing one side of the brain. And he wanted me to perform the surgery, even though I had never done one before.

"Let me get hold of some of the literature and read up on it, and then I'll give you an answer," I told him.

Beginning that day, I read everything I could get my hands on and learned that the procedure had a high complication and mortality rate. Then I stud-ied Maranda's CT scans and medical records and concluded it was at least worth bringing Maranda in to evaluate her. When her parents brought her in, I was struck by how pretty this little girl was, but I also felt such a heaviness for the child. All that suf-fering—and now I might be her only hope. After evaluating her, I decided to go ahead with the sur-gery, but first I needed to explain the risks to Terry (Luis had flown back to his job as a grocery-store manager).

"Maranda could die in the operating room," I gently explained. "She could bleed to death during surgery, and even if she survives the operation, she could be paralyzed and never speak again. On the other hand, she might do very well and never have another seizure."

Terry received this calmly, then looked me straight in the eye and asked, "And what if we don't consent to the surgery?"

I had to be truthful: "She'll get worse and die."

"Then please, operate."

On the night before the surgery, Luis flew back, and I met with both parents once again to explain the risks their daughter would face the next day. I wanted to be absolutely sure they knew what could happen—that they might not see their daughter alive again.

"Dr. Carson," Luis began, "we know the risks. But this is our only chance."

As I stood to leave, I said to the parents, "Now I have a homework assignment for you. I give this to every patient and family member before surgery."

"Anything," Terry said.

"Say your prayers. I think that really does help." And I really believe that. While I stay away from religious discussions with patients, I like to remind them of God's loving presence. Just as I need to remind myself, for as I left to go home and get some sleep, the weight of the next day fell heavy on my shoulders. Maranda's life would be in my hands. But I took comfort in knowing that the Lord would never get me into something he couldn't get me out of.

"God," I prayed, "if Maranda dies, she dies, but we'll know that we've done the best we could for her." With that thought I had peace and went to sleep.

CHAPTER 16

They're More Than Patients

Assisted by Dr. Neville Knuckey, one of our chief residents, I began with an incision down the scalp. Then I cut deeper through a second layer of scalp before drilling six holes, each the size of a shirt button, in Maranda's skull. The holes formed a semicircle, beginning in front of her left ear and curving up across her temple, above and behind the ear. Then with an air-powered saw I connected the holes into an incision and lifted back the left side of Maranda's skull to expose the outer covering of her brain.

Right from the beginning we had problems. Maranda's brain was severely inflamed so that wherever an instrument touched, she started to bleed. We had to keep calling for blood as Maranda lost nearly nine pints during the surgery. Her brain was swollen and abnormally hard, stretching the anticipated four-hour procedure into eight hours. Slowly, carefully I inched away the inflamed left hemisphere of her brain, the small surgical instruments moving carefully, a millimeter at a time as I coaxed tissue away from the vital blood vessels. It wasn't easy to manipulate the brain, to ease it away from the veins that circulated life through her small body, and I needed to make sure I didn't touch or damage the other parts of her brain. I thanked God for his wisdom and for helping guide my hands.

Finally, we were finished. The OR technician took the last instrument from my hand as I looked down at Maranda. We had successfully removed the left hemisphere of her brain, but it remained to be seen if she would ever walk or talk again. Neville and I stepped back as another aide removed Maranda from the ventilator. She began breathing on her own but did not respond as a nurse called her name. *She'll wake up soon,* I told myself. But would she?

I followed Maranda's gurney as she was wheeled down the hall to the pediatric intensive care unit. Her eyes were swollen from being under the anesthesia for so long, and her lips were puffy from having a respirator tube down her throat for ten hours. She looked vulnerable, even grotesque.

The Franciscos had spent more than ten hours in the waiting room, and as soon as they heard the gurney, they ran out to meet us.

"Please wait," Terry called softly, her eyes red-rimmed, her face pale.

She went to the gurney, bent over, and kissed her daughter. Maranda's eyes fluttered open briefly.

"I love you, Mommy and Daddy."

I just stood there, amazed and excited. We had hoped for a recovery, but no one dared to think she would recover so quickly. We had removed the left side of her brain, the dominant part that controls speech, yet Maranda was talking. She stretched her right leg and moved her right arm—the side controlled by the half of the brain we removed. Word quickly spread, and the whole staff ran toward us to witness this amazing turn of events. Amidst the exclamations, I heard a woman's voice say, "Praise the Lord!"

Since her surgery, Maranda has had no more seizures. She enrolled in tap-dancing classes and even appeared on the *Phil Donahue Show*. It wasn't long before others approached me to perform this procedure, which had once been looked upon so skeptically by the medical profession. Other hospitals also started doing them—by the end of 1988, surgeons at UCLA had done six. In all, I think I did around sixty, but none struck me as deeply as the one I performed on eleven-month-old Jennifer.

Based on what I discovered from doing EEGs, CT scans, and MRIs, I decided to remove only the back part of baby Jennifer's right hemisphere. The surgery seemed successful, but shortly after recovery, she began having seizures again. We took her back into the OR, where I removed the remaining part of the right hemisphere, and again, everything seemed to go just fine. Exhausted, I got in my car for the thirty-five-minute drive home, and just before reaching my house, my beeper went off. This was before cell phones, so I raced home, ran into the house, and called the hospital. "Shortly after you left, Jennifer arrested. They're resuscitating her now."

I hopped back in my car and made it back to the hospital in twenty minutes, praying all the way: *Please God, don't let Jennifer die*. When I got to her bed in the pediatric ICU, I looked at the nurse, and her eyes said what I already knew. Jennifer wasn't coming back. I hurried to the room where her parents waited and began, "I'm sorry ..." That's as far as I got. For the first time in my adult life I began crying in public. Like all the others, Jennifer was more than a patient to me. You almost become part of their family. Her parents had gone through so much, only to lose their only child. As a surgeon, the hardest task I have is facing parents with bad news about their child. Every time a patient dies, I carry another emotional scar.

I didn't believe in remaining emotionally detached from my patients. I worked with and operated on human beings, all creatures of God, people in pain who needed help. And whenever I operated and things did not go well, I felt a keen responsibility for the outcome. I understood the risks involved in the work I did, but I also knew that sometimes avoiding those wasn't an option.

CHAPTER 17

Never Give Up on Life

Performing brain surgery is always risky, but sometimes the risks are so great that it made sense to some of my respected colleagues just not to do the operation. But it didn't always make sense to me. Such was the case with little four-year-old Bo-Bo Valentine.

After being hit by a car as she ran across a street, Bo-Bo had been rushed to our ICU, where now she lay comatose. When I visited her on my rounds, the house officer explained her condition. He said, "Just about the only thing she has left is pupillary response," meaning that her pupils responded to light.

But when I bent over her and lifted her eyelids, her pupils were fixed and dilated.

"Four-plus emergency," I called loudly but calmly. "Call the operating room. We're on our way."

Although rare, a four-plus is a dire emergency, galvanizing everyone into a carefully choreographed response. Even as two residents grabbed Bo-Bo's bed and raced down the hallway, the OR staff was getting the instruments ready. On my way to the OR I ran into another neurosurgeon—a man I highly respected—and explained what had happened and what I was going to do.

"Don't do it," he cautioned as he walked away from me. "You're wasting your time."

I could hardly believe what I had just heard. Bo-Bo Valentine was still alive. We had a chance, though extremely small. A chance to save a child's life. I decided to go ahead with the surgery.

Bo-Bo was gently placed on the operating table, and within minutes, the nurse and anesthesiologist signaled that she was ready. I opened her head and removed the front portion of her skull, placing it in a sterile solution. Then I opened the covering of the brain, the dura, and split the falx, an area between the brain's two hemispheres, which equalized the pressure. I then sewed cadaveric dura (dura from a dead person) over her brain, giving it room to swell without causing damage. If it worked, we would bring her back in and replace the section of her skull that I had removed. If it didn't?

After two days of lying in a coma, Bo-Bo started moving a little. Over the course of a week, she grew more responsive. Relieved, we took her back to surgery and replaced the missing portion of her skull. Within six weeks Bo-Bo was once again a normal four-year-old girl.

And I was glad I hadn't let my colleague's opinion influence my decision to try to save a child's life.

Sometimes, however, it was not a colleague who wanted to give up, but a more unlikely obstacle: a parent. In the summer of 1988, I had to explain to a distraught mother that the only hope for her ten-year-old son was to remove a portion of his brain. He too had been struck by a car; his condition was worse than Bo-Bo's.

"Absolutely not," she cried. "You're not going to play around with my kid. Just let him die!"

Of course, I understood how she felt. We couldn't promise her that this radical procedure would work. Earlier she had been told that her son would never recover, so from her perspective, we were just using him as an experiment. Desperate to convince her, I shared Bo-Bo's story, adding, "I don't see how we can give up in a situation where we still have even a glimmer of hope."

She signed the consent form, and we rushed her son into surgery. I essentially performed the same surgery as I had with Bo-Bo, but after a week, he still remained comatose. I began hearing things like "ballgame's over" from staff members. During our neurosurgical grand rounds, a colleague presented the boy's case because I couldn't be there. I learned later that my fellow surgeons were pretty rough on me.

"Isn't this going a bit beyond the call of duty?" one asked.

"The patient hasn't recovered, and he's not *going* to recover," another offered.

They weren't being unkind—just doing their job. This type of criticism was designed to help all of us make better decisions. And since the boy hadn't recovered after seven days, their skepticism was understandable. Maybe it's because I'm stubborn, or maybe I have a hard time giving up when a life is at stake. But I still had hope.

On the eighth day, his eyelids fluttered. It was Bo-Bo all over again, except that his recovery had taken longer. It would have been perfectly acceptable for me to have honored his mother's initial request to let her son die. But I'm glad I didn't. And she is too.

Not all such decisions have happy endings, but as I look back, I have no regrets taking on cases that others considered hopeless. Once, after a tedious nineteen-hour surgery, when I tag-teamed with another surgeon on a four-month old girl, she began to show signs of recovering, only to die in ICU. Her mother's words explain why I find it so hard to give up: "We know that you're a man of God and that the Lord has all these things in his hands. Despite this outcome, we'll always be grateful for everything that was done here."

CHAPTER 18

"Remember What Your Mother Said"

I headed to the room of a patient on whom I would operate that day, and I found myself in a prayer meeting. My patient, named Craig Warnick, and his wife, Susan, a nurse at Johns Hopkins, were Christians and had been joined by twenty-five to thirty friends who had gathered to pray for the next day's surgery. I stayed a few minutes and prayed too. When I left the room, Susan followed me into the hallway.

"Don't forget what your mother said," she smiled.

"I won't," I answered, remembering that I had once shared my mom's words with her: "Bennie, if you ask the Lord for something, believing he will do it, then he will do it."

As I contemplated Craig's surgery, I knew those words would be put to good use because the tumor I would try to remove was on his brain stem—an area considered inoperable. But it was Craig's only hope. Ever since he was a senior in high school, he had suffered from a rare disease known as Von Hippel-Lindau, or VHL. By the time he was twenty-two he had undergone lung surgery, an adrenalectomy, and two brain-tumor resections, and had experienced tumors of the retinas. After his first surgery, he had trouble with his balance and with swallowing, symptoms that never really left him. After so many surgeries with so little improvement, Craig was physically miserable, emotionally depressed, and ready to give up.

Yet despite all of these setbacks, he graduated from college shortly after marrying Susan, who proceeded to become an expert in VHL. She researched everything she could get her hands on. Oh yes—in addition to caring for Craig and studying VHL, she earned her nurse's degree and began working at Johns Hopkins, which is how I got to know her. I learned that they were high school sweethearts—Susan once said she believed from the beginning that they had a special, heaven-sent love. They both became Christians in high school through the ministry of Young Life and were active members of their church.

When Craig developed yet another tumor—the one on his brain stem—Craig and Susan must not have heard the word *inoperable* because they asked me if I would operate. I was already backed up with patients and had no room on my schedule, so I recommended one of the other neurosurgeons at Johns Hopkins.

"We'd really like you to do it," Craig said in his quiet voice.

"If there's any way possible," Susan added. "We know how busy you are and ..."

I managed to convince them to transfer to the other surgeon's care, but as it turned out, he didn't think the procedure he had planned to use would work on Craig's particular type of tumor. In the meantime, Craig's condition deteriorated rapidly, and he was admitted to the emergency room. Susan called me, and as I listened to the worry and concern in her voice, I knew I had to do something.

"Okay, I'm going to reschedule tomorrow's patient. We'll get Craig into surgery."

We scheduled him for the next day, so I had to go over the risks with Craig and Susan that night. I explained that I wouldn't know how to proceed until I got inside his brain to investigate. "If it's in the brain stem ..." I paused.

"We understand," Craig answered.

"It's going to be all right," Susan added.

I went home that night grateful for her encouragement, and it was the next day that I happened upon the prayer meeting in Craig's room. Within a few hours I was in the OR, trying to find the tumor in Craig's brain. First I used a microscope to locate it, but I couldn't find anything except that his brain stem was badly swollen. It had to be in there somewhere, so next I stuck a needle into the brain stem, which only provoked excessive bleeding. It was a tough operation, and after eight hours we closed Craig up and sent him back to the ICU, somewhat anxious that all that poking around might have caused major complications.

To my surprise, Craig was making jokes when I visited him the next day. I was glad he was in good spirits, because the news I had for him might be hard to take. I explained that I thought his tumor was in the middle of the pons—part of the brain stem—and that I was just too tired the previous night to try and remove it. "I'm willing to open up the pons, but there's at least a 50-50 chance that you'll die on the operating table. And if you survive, you could be paralyzed or devastated neurologically."

Their confidence was incredible.

"Do it," Craig insisted.

"We're praying for a miracle," Susan added. "We believe God is going to do it through you."

In the operating room, it was tough going. I always pray before operating, but this time I was acutely conscious of praying during the entire surgery. Once inside, every time I touched the brain stem with an instrument, it began bleeding profusely. *What do I do now?* I prayed. *God, help me know what to do.*

I knew that unless I could get inside the brain stem, Craig would die. Then, in an instant, I intuitively knew what to do. "Hand me the laser," I said to the technician.

Using the laser, I cautiously opened a tiny hole in the brain stem, and the beam coagulated some of the bleeding vessels as I went in. I then teased out a tiny piece of the tumor, but it was stuck. I tugged gently, but nothing came out. By this time the anesthesiologist informed me that there were no brain waves on one side of Craig's brain—a sign of severe damage.

"We're in here; we're going to keep going," I announced to my team, then breathed another prayer. *God, I just can't give up. Please guide my hands.*

I kept at the hole in the stem, my hands pulling gently. Finally, the tumorous growth started coming out, and as I tugged it, all of a sudden, it came free in one gigantic blob. Obviously, I was pleased, but in the back of my mind I wondered how much damage I'd done to Craig's brain.

The next day on my rounds I stopped by Craig's room, and once again I couldn't believe what I saw. Craig was sitting up in bed. I performed a few routine tests, and everything was normal. He still had problems swallowing, but everything else seemed okay.

"You got your miracle, Craig," I told him.

"I know," he said, his face glowing.

CHAPTER 19

An Impossible Assignment

Despite wanting to kill herself when she discovered she was carrying Siamese twins, once Theresa Binder gave birth, she immediately fell in love with Patrick and Benjamin. Theresa and her husband, Josef, learned to hold their babies, joined at the head, to be sure they were both well supported. They lived with the hope that their chubby blond sons would one day be separated, but because the boys shared a major vein responsible for draining blood from the brain and returning it to the heart, such hope was unfounded. No one had successfully separated Siamese twins joined at the back of the cranium with both surviving.

The Binders lived in Germany, and their babies' physicians contacted Johns Hopkins to see if we might accept this daunting challenge. After studying the available information, I tentatively agreed to the surgery, knowing it would be the riskiest and most demanding thing I had ever done. Dr. Mark Rodgers, director of Pediatric Intensive Care, coordinated the massive undertaking, which included seven anesthesiologists, five neurosurgeons, two cardiac surgeons, five plastic surgeons, and dozens of nurses and technicians—seventy people in all.

For five months, we planned the surgery, working out where each person would stand and creating a ten-page play-by-play book detailing every step of the operation. Additionally, we conducted five three-hour dress rehearsals, using life-sized dolls attached at the head by Velcro. Finally, we were ready. I would do the actual separating, then Dr. Donlin Long would work on one boy while I took the other; the best qualified medical team would be alongside, ready to jump in when their specialty was needed. On Saturday, September 5, 1987, we began operating on the seven-month-old twins.

Before I could separate them, we had to induce a deep degree of hypothermia, which allowed us to stop the heart and blood flow for approximately one hour without causing brain damage. Just before 11:30 p.m., I severed the thin blue main vein in the back of the twins' heads that carried blood out of the brain. For the first time in their lives, Patrick and Benjamin were living apart from each other. But Dr. Long and I had to work quickly as we began fashioning a new vein from pieces of pericardium (the covering of the heart) that had been removed earlier. If we went beyond the allotted time, the boys would either die or suffer permanent brain damage.

Shortly into the process of reconstructing the huge vein on my twin, I hit a snag. I would need much more time than scheduled. Blood rushed through the vein under such pressure that even a tiny hole would cause the baby to bleed to death in less than a minute once we allowed the blood to return to their little bodies. Fortunately the cardio-vascular surgeons were looking over our shoulders and cut pieces of the pericardium exactly the right diameter and shape. They fit perfectly, and we were able to sew them into place.

At the forty-five minute mark, I knew we were getting close to our deadline. The tension level increased. I could sense everyone thinking, *Are we going to finish in time?* Dr. Long completed his baby first, and I completed mine within seconds before the blood started to flow again. We made it!

Or so we thought.

Once we started the infants' hearts, all the tiny vessels that had been severed during surgery began bleeding profusely. We spent the next three hours trying everything to stop the bleeding, going through pints of blood in the process. When we learned that we were almost out of our blood supply, six or eight people volunteered to donate their own blood. Fortunately, our blood bank called the Red Cross, and they were able to provide enough for us to continue. In all, we used sixty pints of blood—several dozen times the boys' normal blood volume.

Eventually we finished, and the plastic-surgery team went to work sewing their scalps back together. Now, the long wait to see if the twins would recover. We had been at it for twenty-two hours.

For ten days, Patrick and Benjamin remained in a medically induced coma to keep the intracranial pressures down. In the middle of the second week, we decided to lighten up the coma, and when I stopped by to check on them, I noticed movement.

"They're moving!" someone exclaimed. "They're going to make it."

We were overjoyed. But what about their neurological functions? That same day, as the barbiturates wore off, both boys opened their eyes and started looking around. I couldn't believe this was happening. I hadn't expected them to survive twenty-four hours, yet here they were, progressing beyond my wildest dreams.

Though we encountered some setbacks along the way, Patrick and Benjamin, week by week, started doing more things and interacting positively. The postoperative care was as spectacular as the surgery—we had all become a wonderful, marvelous team. And the twins? Because of a contractual agreement between the parents and a German magazine, I am unable to share the rest of their story. But I do know one thing: the two were separated, and the much-loved twin boys celebrated their second birthday together.

Thank you, God. Thank you! I know you had your hand in this.

CHAPTER 20

What about You?

I've shared my story not so much to draw attention to myself, but to encourage everyone —especially disadvantaged young people—to believe that they can achieve whatever dreams and goals they have. If a poor black kid from Detroit can make it, anyone can. As I continue to pursue my own dreams, I want to see thousands of deserving people of every age and race moving into leadership because of their talents and commitments.

My passion for young people traces its origins to that summer when I worked as a recruiter for Yale. How sad to see so many kids who wanted to go to college but had no chance because their SAT scores were so low. I could see that these were bright kids, and I recalled my own difficulty taking tests. All they needed was someone who believed in them and could help them overcome the barriers that stood between them and a college entrance exam.

I made a commitment then to accept as many opportunities as I could to encourage people, especially young people. As my story became more well-known, I began receiving invitations to speak at schools and other organizations, and my message was always the same. Set your sights high. Stay focused on your goals. You can be successful in whatever you choose to do. I would hope that, in a way, I was becoming to them what my mother was to me. All those times I heard her say, "Bennie, you can do it!" finally sank in, and now I want to make sure others, especially young people, hear those same encouraging words.

But no one should have to try to do it on their own. We all need others to help us along the way. Young people certainly need parents, guardians, teachers, pastors—responsible adults in their communities—to step up and address their needs. Maybe that's you. Maybe you can be like Mrs. Miller, an English teacher who will take a personal interest in that ninth grader who's struggling in your class. Or Uncle William, opening your home to a child whose parents are going through rough times. Maybe you can volunteer to tutor a fourth-grader. Perhaps you could offer a summer job to a young person trying to save up money for college. If there's one thing you take from my story, I hope it's the fact that with a little of the right kind of help, anyone can turn his or her life around and contribute greatly to society regardless of their age. They just can't do it alone.

In addition to sharing my own story, I try to point young people to successful role models. This is especially important in the African American community where many kids get the impression that their only hope is to become a professional athlete or musician. Unfortunately, the media helps perpetuate that unrealistic dream by heaping adulation on stars who make it to the top with little more than a high school diploma, if that. Out of all the kids who play sports in high school, only a tiny percentage—roughly 0.5 percent, according to the NCAA—make it to the professional level, and sadly, many of them end up broke a few years after their careers end. And for every musician millionaire, thousands struggle in obscurity.

It's important that young people from disadvantaged communities learn about successful men and women who overcame obstacles. People like my friend Fred Wilson, an engineer with Ford Motor Company. Fred is black and was named by Ford as one of their top eight engineers worldwide. I would love to see the media focus more attention on other successful African Americans who are not athletes or musicians. At first, I was surprised at all the attention I got as a neurosurgeon until I realized that to African Americans I represented something that they too could aspire to become—a black person excelling in a technical or scientific field. My experience has led many teenagers to conclude, "Maybe I could do that." When young people have good role models, they can change and set their sights toward higher achievements.

The Bible says that "From everyone who has been given much, much will be demanded" (Luke 12:48). With a lot of help from others, I have been given a wonderful career, a remarkable wife, three great kids, grandchildren, and so much more. These blessings come with an urgent sense of responsibility to give back.

Several years ago, a little fifth-grade boy sat at his desk in a predominately white classroom and silently pronounced, "I'm just dumb." I believed those words and was ready to accept the hopelessness they promised. Thankfully, my mother and a lot of other people believed otherwise. And because they believed in me, I began to believe in myself. It wasn't always easy, and it still isn't. Successful people don't have fewer problems. They simply determine that nothing will stop them from going forward.

I am certain that there are still way too many children and adults who think they are too dumb or too poor or face too many obstacles to become successful. All they need is for someone to tell them, "You can do it!" and show them how.

Maybe that someone is you.

About the Author

D r. Carson is emeritus professor of neurosurgery, oncology, plastic surgery, and pediatrics at the Johns Hopkins School of Medicine. In 1984, he was named director of pediatric neurosurgery at Johns Hopkins Children's Center, a position he retired from in 2013. In 2008, he was named the inaugural recipient of a professorship in his name, the Benjamin S. Carson, Sr., M.D., and Dr. Evelyn Spiro, R.N., Professor of Pediatric Neurosurgery. Also in 2008, he was awarded the Presidential Medal of Freedom, the highest civilian honor in the land. He was the keynote speaker for the President's National Prayer Breakfasts in 1997 and 2013.

Through his philanthropic foundation, the Carson Scholars Fund, he and his wife, Candy, strive to maximize the intellectual potential of every child. An internationally renowned physician, Dr. Carson has authored over a hundred neurosurgical publications and has been awarded more than sixty honorary doctorate degrees and dozens of national merit citations. Dr. Carson has written eight best-selling books, and his fifth book, *America the Beautiful: Rediscovering What Made This Nation Great*, released in early 2012, made the *New York Times* Bestseller List. His sixth book, *One Nation:*

What We Can All Do to Save America's Future, was released in 2014 and became a number one *New York Times* bestseller. He is a syndicated columnist and a highly sought-after, world-renowned inspirational and motivational speaker.

CARSON SCHOLARS FUND

The Carson Scholars Fund supports two main initiatives: **Carson Scholarships** and the **Ben Carson Reading Project.** Our scholarship program awards students who have embraced high levels of academic excellence and community service with $1,000 college scholarships. The Ben Carson Reading Project provides funding to schools to build and maintain Ben Carson Reading Rooms—warm, inviting rooms where children can discover the joy of independent leisure reading.

Through the generosity of our donors and partners, we are able to award more than 500 scholarships annually. In total, we have awarded over 4,800 scholarships across the country. Our scholars come from all across the country, and our award winners currently represent forty-five states and the District of Columbia. Carson Scholarship winners have attended more than 300 colleges and universities, and have received nearly $2 million in scholarship funds to help finance their education.

To learn more about Dr. Ben Carson and Carson Scholars Fund, visit http://carsonscholars.org/.

ZONDERVAN®
.com

America the Beautiful

Rediscovering What Made This Nation Great

Ben Carson, MD with Candy Carson

What is America becoming? Or, more importantly, what can she be if we reclaim a vision for the things that made her great in the first place?

In America the Beautiful, Dr. Ben Carson helps us learn from our past in order to chart a better course for our future.

From his personal ascent from inner-city poverty to international medical and humanitarian acclaim, Carson shares experiential insights that help us understand
... what is good about America
... where we have gone astray
... which fundamental beliefs have guided America from her founding into preeminence among nations

Written by a man who has experienced America's best and worst firsthand, America the Beautiful is at once alarming, convicting, and inspiring. You'll gain new perspectives on our nation's origins, our Judeo-Christian heritage, our educational system, capitalism versus socialism, our moral fabric, healthcare, and much more.

An incisive manifesto of the values that shaped America's past and must shape her future, America the Beautiful calls us all to use our God-given talents to improve our lives, our communities, our nation, and our world.

Available in stores and online!

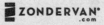

Gifted Hands

The Ben Carson Story

Ben Carson, MD, with Cecil Murphey

Dr. Ben Carson is known around the world for breakthroughs in neurosurgery that have brought hope where no hope existed. In Gifted Hands, he tells of his inspiring odyssey from his childhood in inner-city Detroit to his position as director of pediatric neurosurgery at John Hopkins Medical Institutions at age thirty-three. Taking you into the operating room where he has saved countless lives, Ben Carson is a role model for anyone who attempts the seemingly impossible.

Filled with fascinating case histories, this bestselling book tells the dramatic and intimate story of Ben Carson's struggle to beat the odds—and of the faith and genius that make him one of today's greatest life-givers.

Available in stores and online!

The Big Picture

Getting Perspective on What's Really Important

Ben Carson, MD with Gregg Lewis

Dr. Ben Carson is known as the originator of ground-breaking surgical procedures, a doctor who turn impossible hopes into joyous realities. He is known as well as a compassionate humanitarian who reaches beyond corporate boardrooms to touch the lives of inner-city kids.

What drives him? *The Big Picture*. A vision of something truly worth living for, something that calls forth the best of his amazing talents, energy, and focus.

In *The Big Picture*, Dr. Carson shares with you the overarching philosophy that has shaped his life, causing him to rise from failure to far-reaching influence. This book is not about HOW to succeed—it's about WHY to succeed. It's about broadening your perspectives. It's about finding a vision for your own life that can reframe your priorities, energize your efforts, and inspire you to change the world around you.

Available in stores and online!

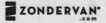

Think Big

Unleashing Your Potential for Excellence

Ben Carson, MD with Cecil Murphey

This book is for you if you have no dreams at all. It's for you if you've bought the lie that you'll never amount to anything. That's not true. Your life is BIG—far bigger than you've imagined.

Inside these pages lie the keys to recognizing the full potential of your life. You won't necessarily become a millionaire (though you might), but you will attain a life that is rewarding, significant, and more fruitful than you ever thought possible.

The author of this book knows about hardship. Ben Carson grew up in inner-city Detroit. His mother was illiterate. His father had left the family. His grade-school classmates considered Ben stupid. He struggled with a violent temper. In every respect, Ben's harsh circumstances seemed only to point to a harsher future and a bad end. But that's not what happened.

By applying the principles in this book, Ben rose from his tough life to one of amazing accomplishments and international renown. He learned that he had potential, he learned how to unleash it, and he did.

You can too. Put the principles in this book in motion. Things won't change overnight, but they will change. You can transform your life into one you'll love, bigger than you've ever dreamed.

Available in stores and online!

Take the Risk

Learning to Identify, Choose, and Live with Acceptable Risk

Ben Carson MD, with Gregg Lewis

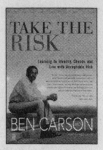

You can find our culture's obsession with avoiding risk everywhere, from multiple insurance policies to crash-tested vehicles. In our 21st-century world, we insulate ourselves with safety. We insure everything from vacations to cell phones. We go on low-cholesterol diets and buy low-risk mutual funds. But is ducking risk the most productive way for us to live? In the end, everyone faces risk. Have we so muffled our hearts and minds that we fail to reach for all that life can offer us—and all that we can offer life? Surgeon and author Dr. Ben Carson, who faces risk on a daily basis, offers an inspiring message in *Take the Risk* on how accepting risk can lead us to a higher purpose.

Available in stores and online!